Art for Your Heart ™

 I0468162

Memories of the 1970s

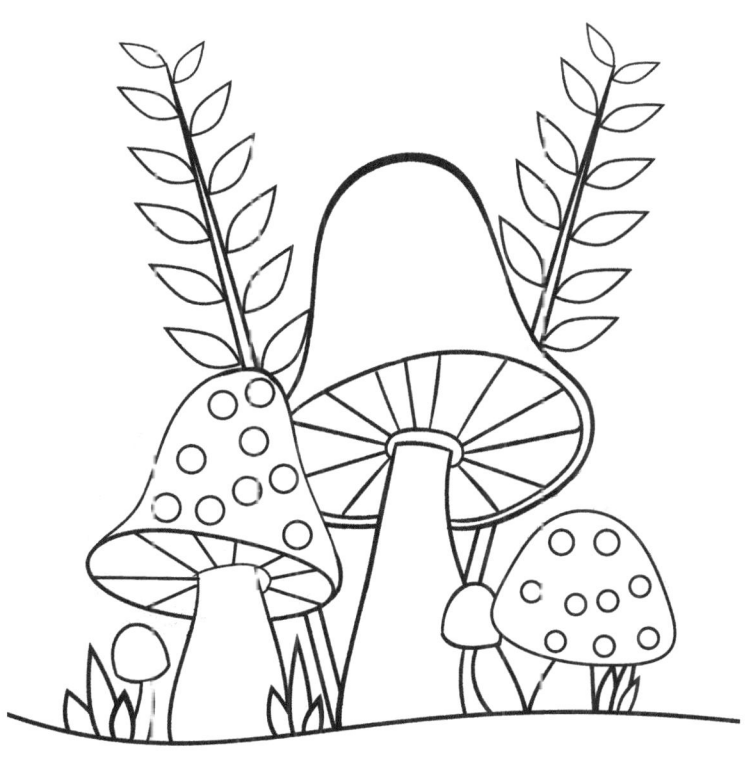

by Alisa Whitley

© 2016 Alisa Whitley
All images © 2016 Alisa Whitley

All rights reserved. No part of this publication may be reproduced, distributed, or transmitted in any form or by any means, including photocopying, recording, or other electronic or mechanical methods, without the prior written permission of the publisher, except in the case of brief quotations embodied in reviews and certain other noncommercial uses permitted by copyright law. For permission requests, contact the author at alisa@alisawhitley.com.

Cover and Interior Design: Alisa Whitley
Visit the author's website at www.alisawhitley.com
Art for Your Heart ™ is a trademark of Alisa Whitley.

First Printing, 2016

10 9 8 7 6 5 4 3 2 1

ISBN 13: 978-1530995929
ISBN: 1530995922

To All of the "children of the 1970s" who thought it was the *best decade ever* in which to grow up!

Peace

Love

Happiness

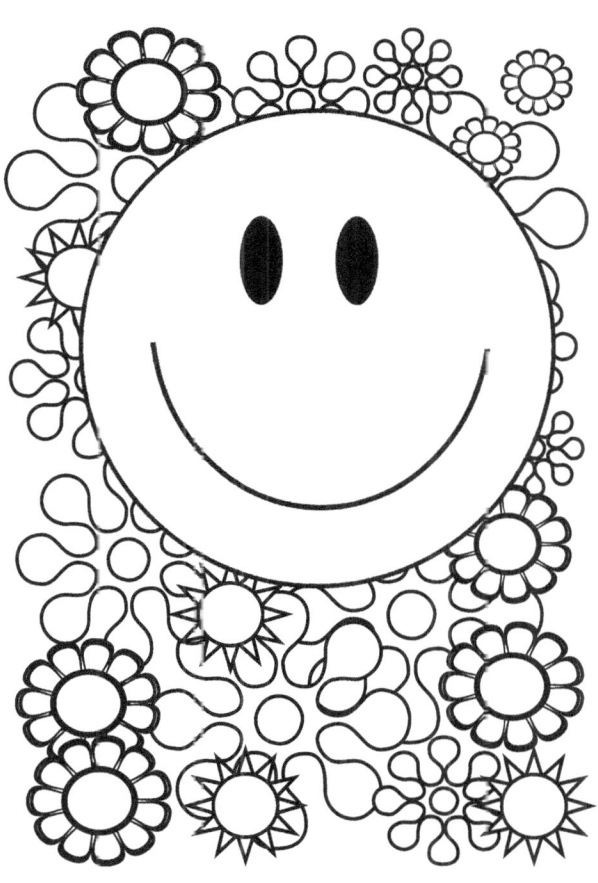

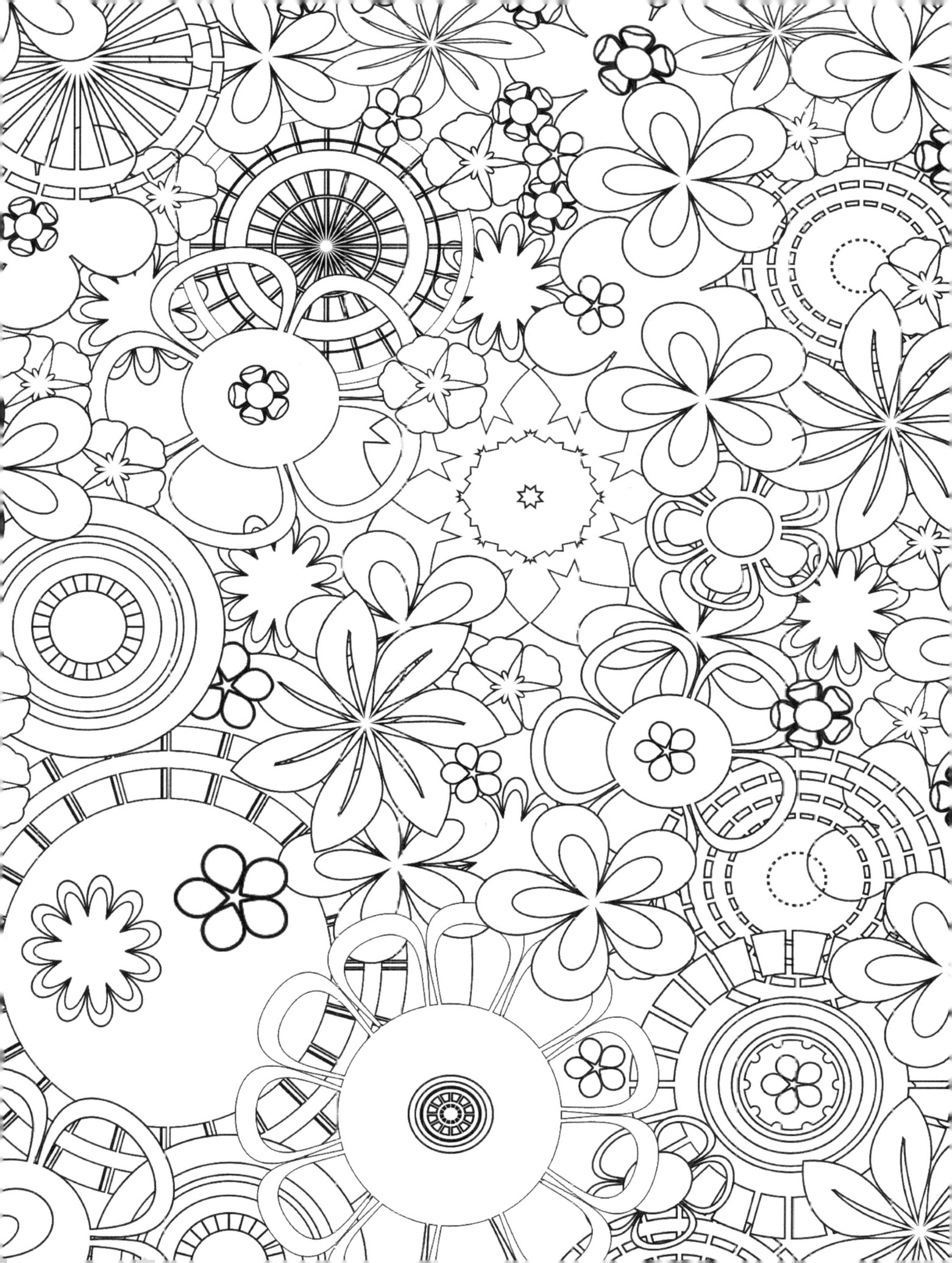

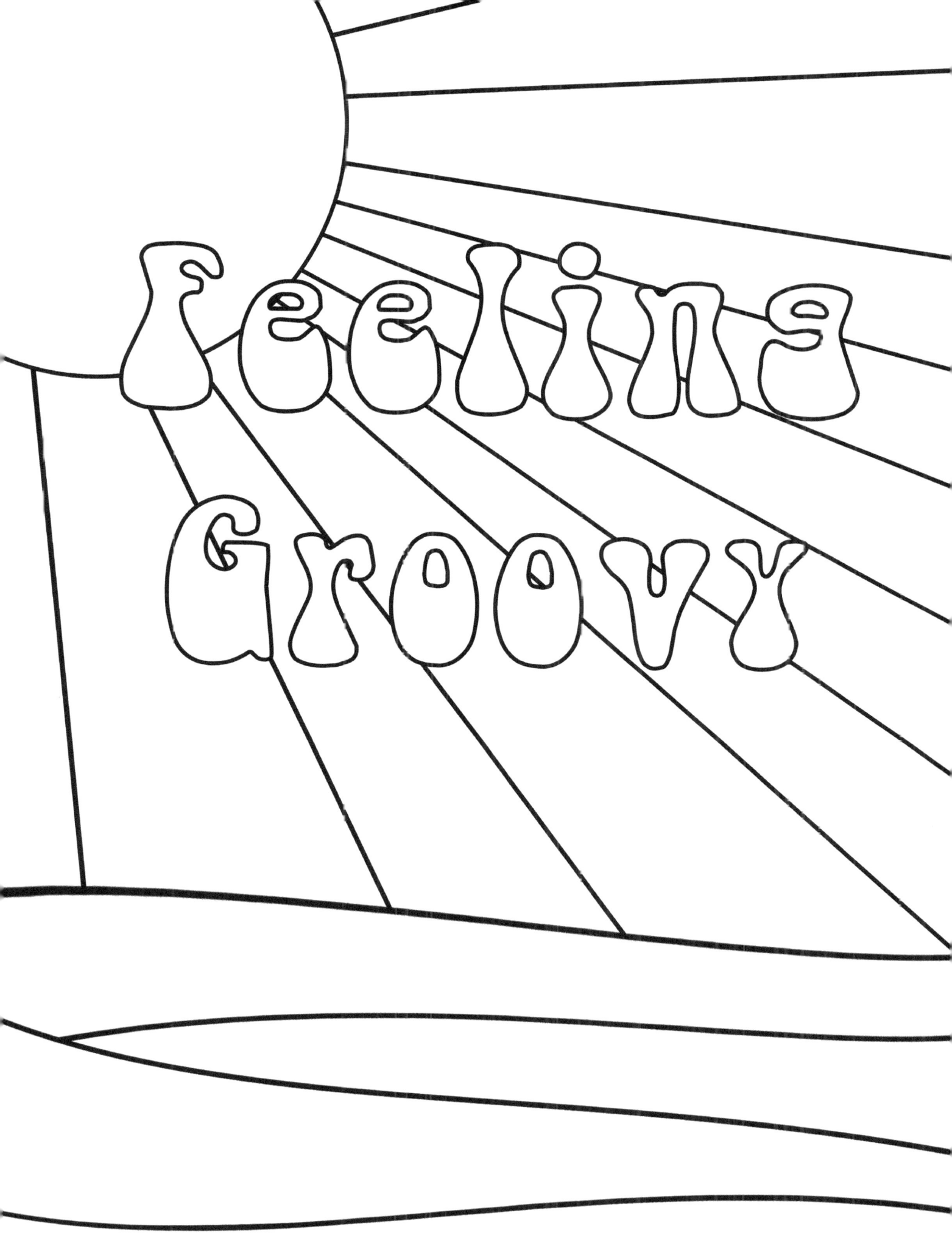

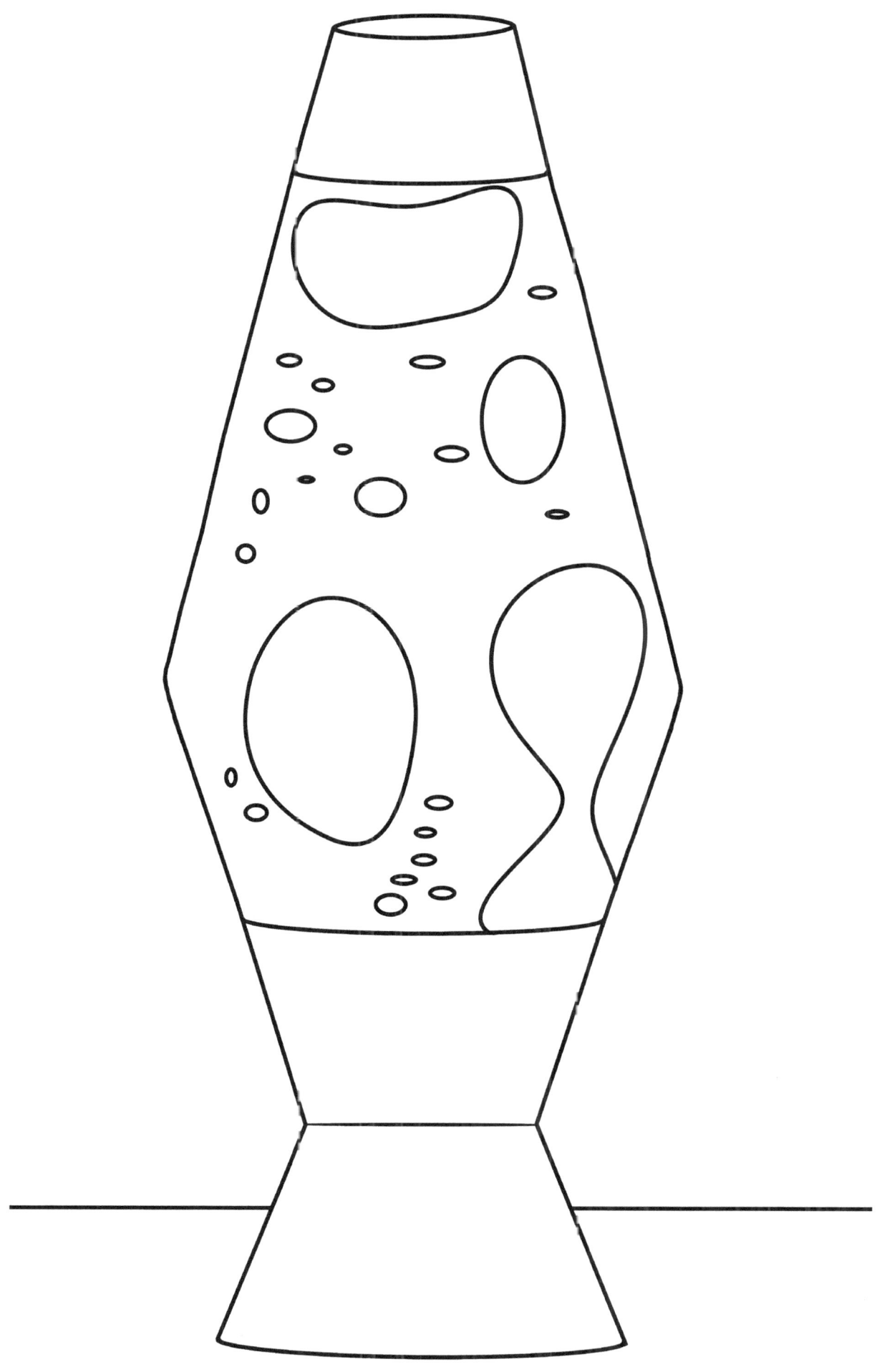

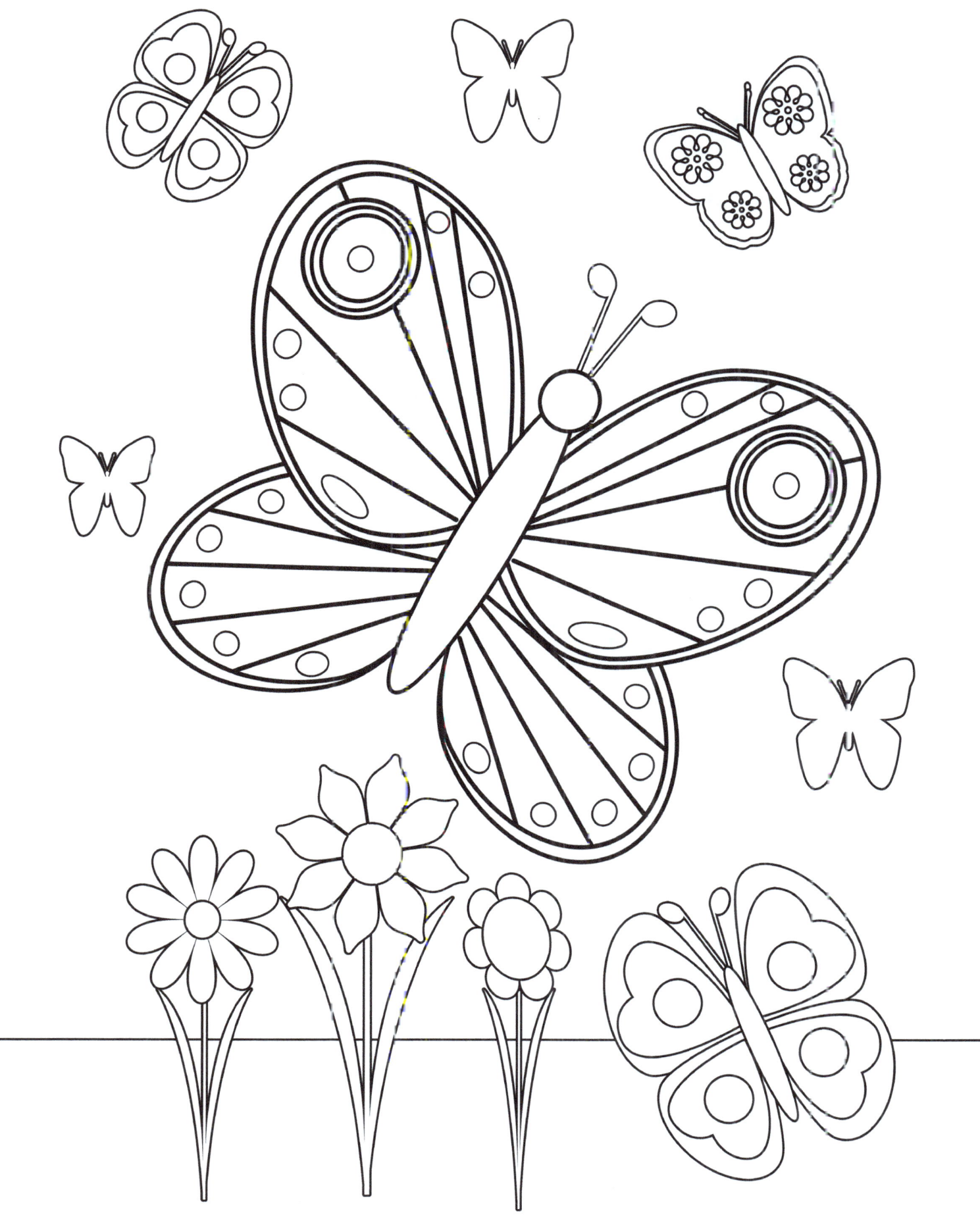

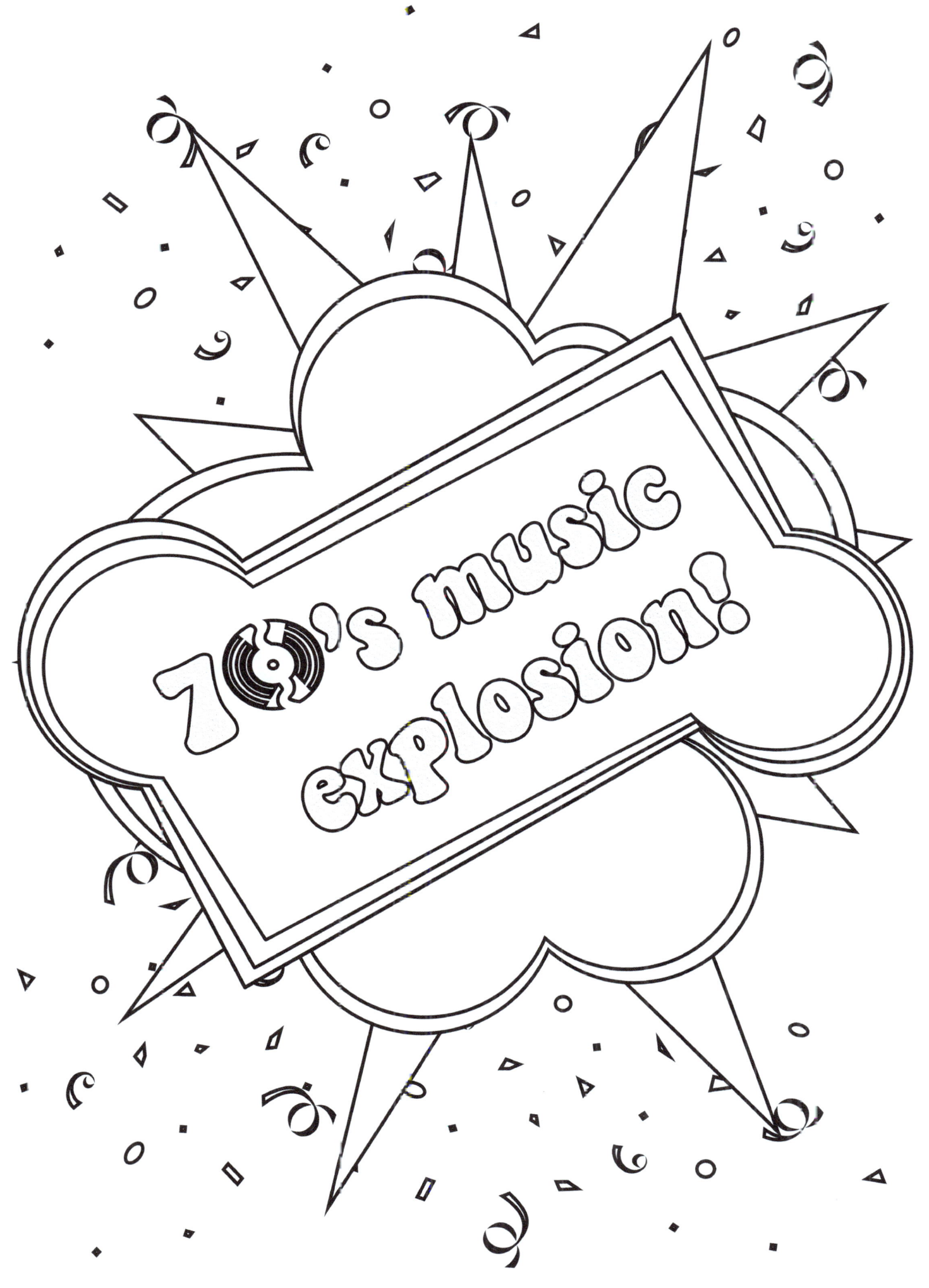

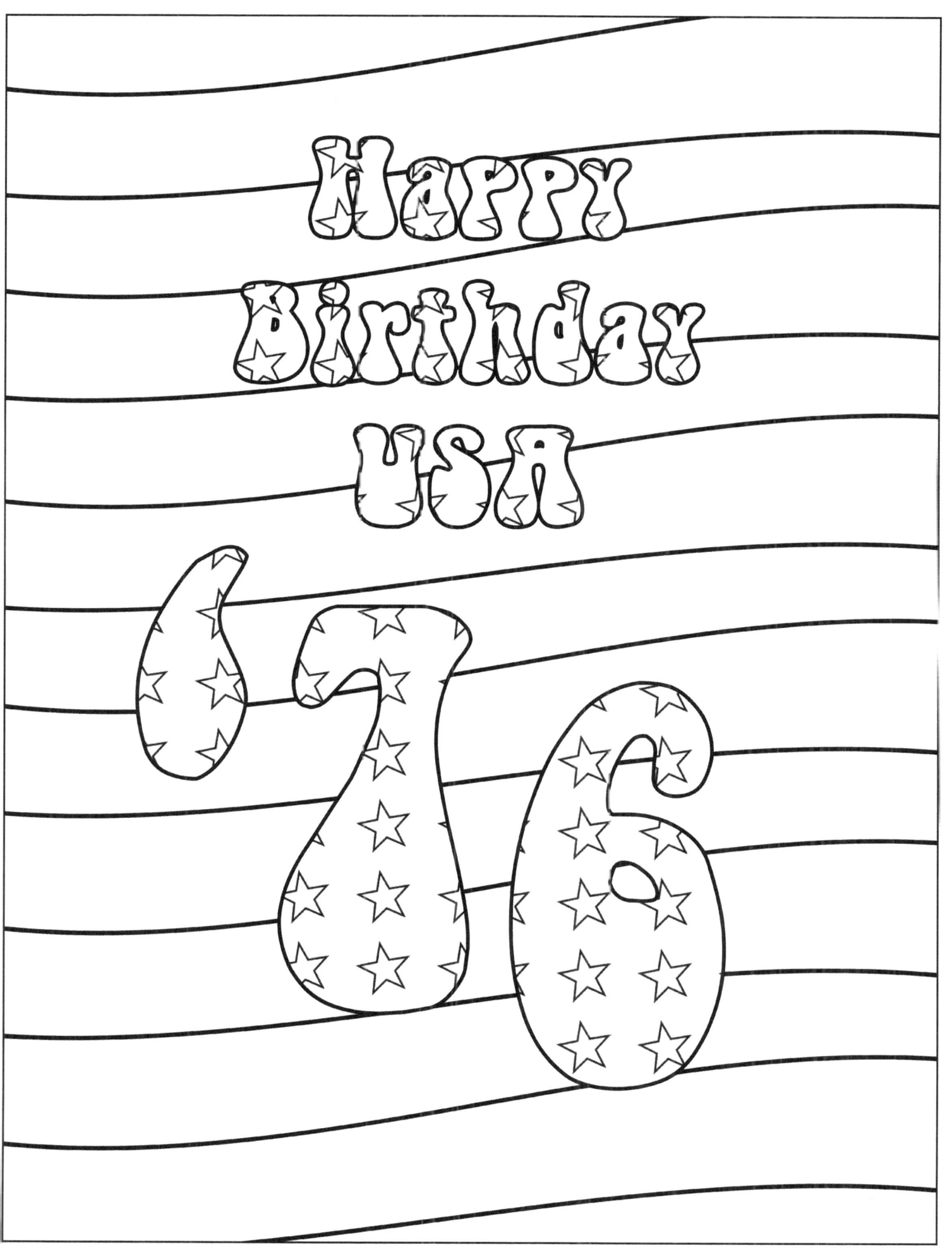

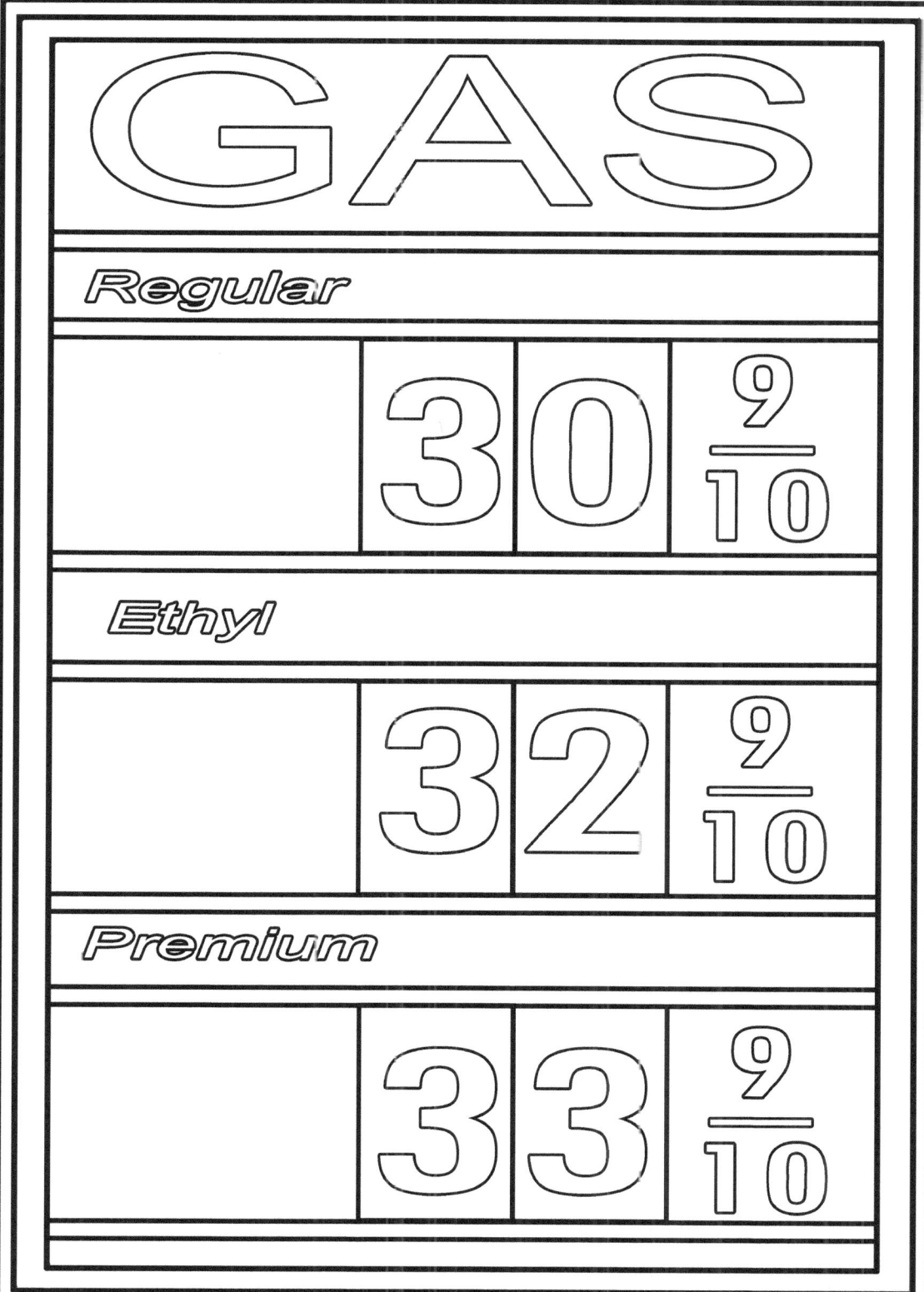

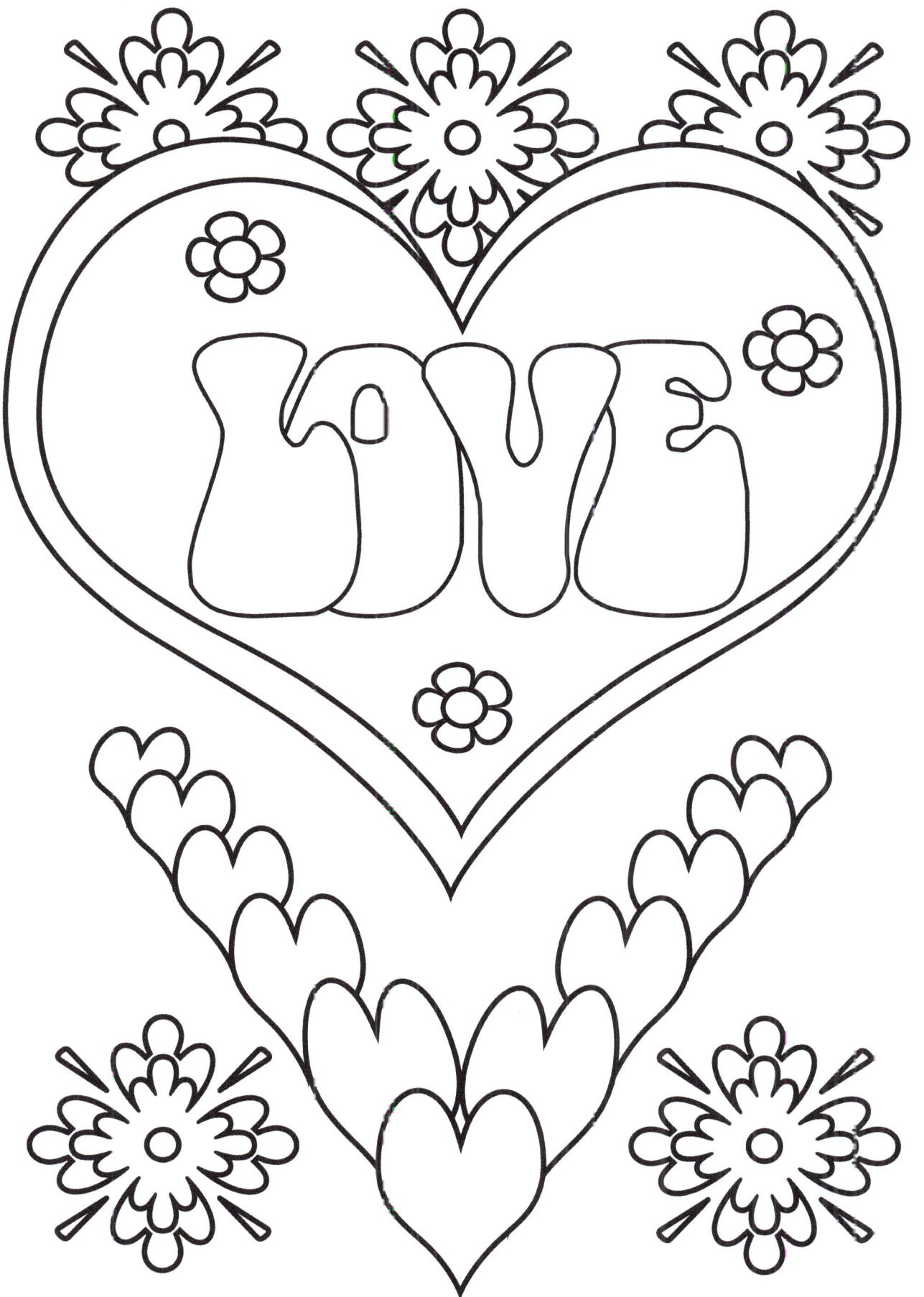

Groovy
Groovy
Groovy
Groovy
Groovy

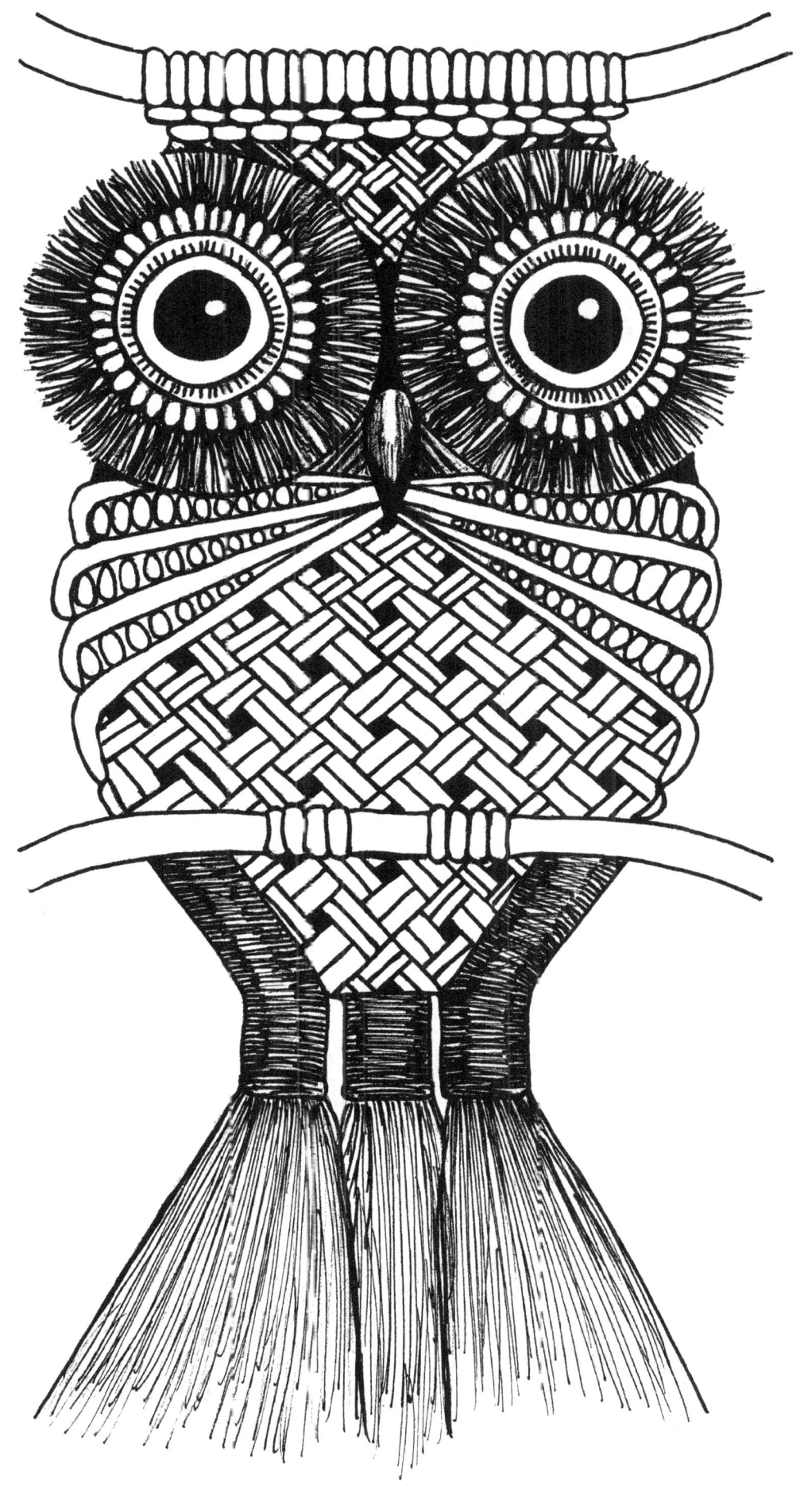

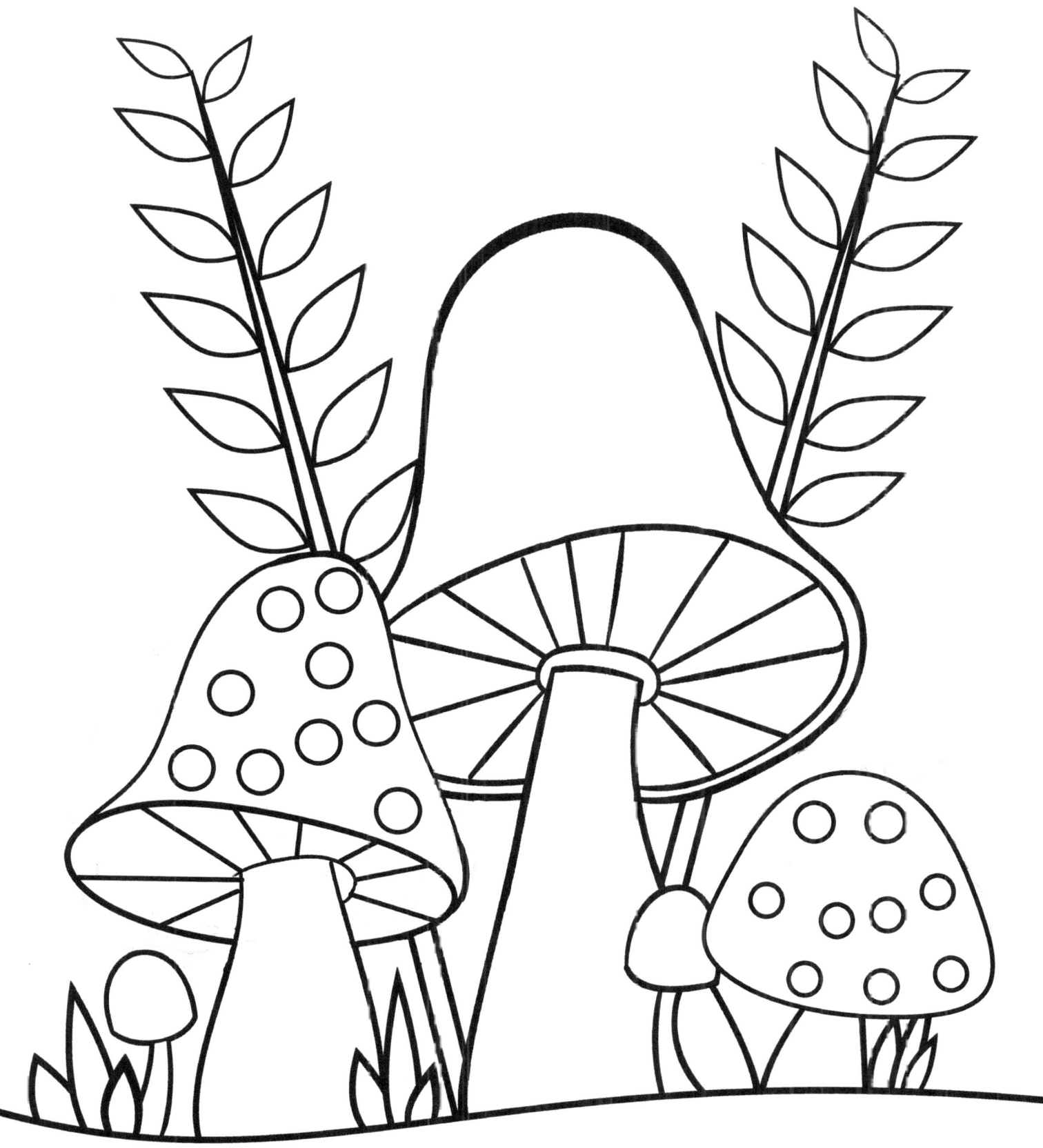

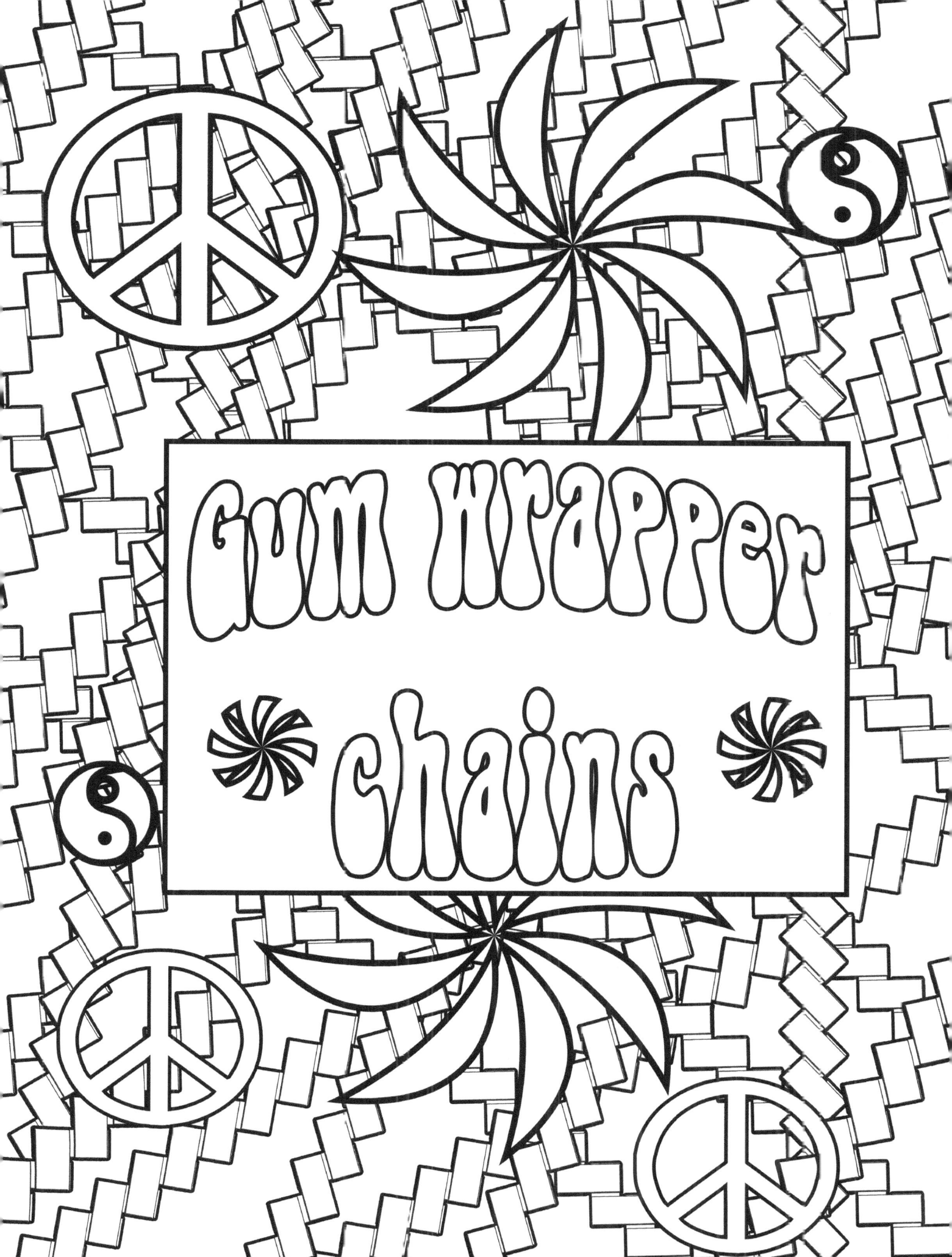

Mood Rings

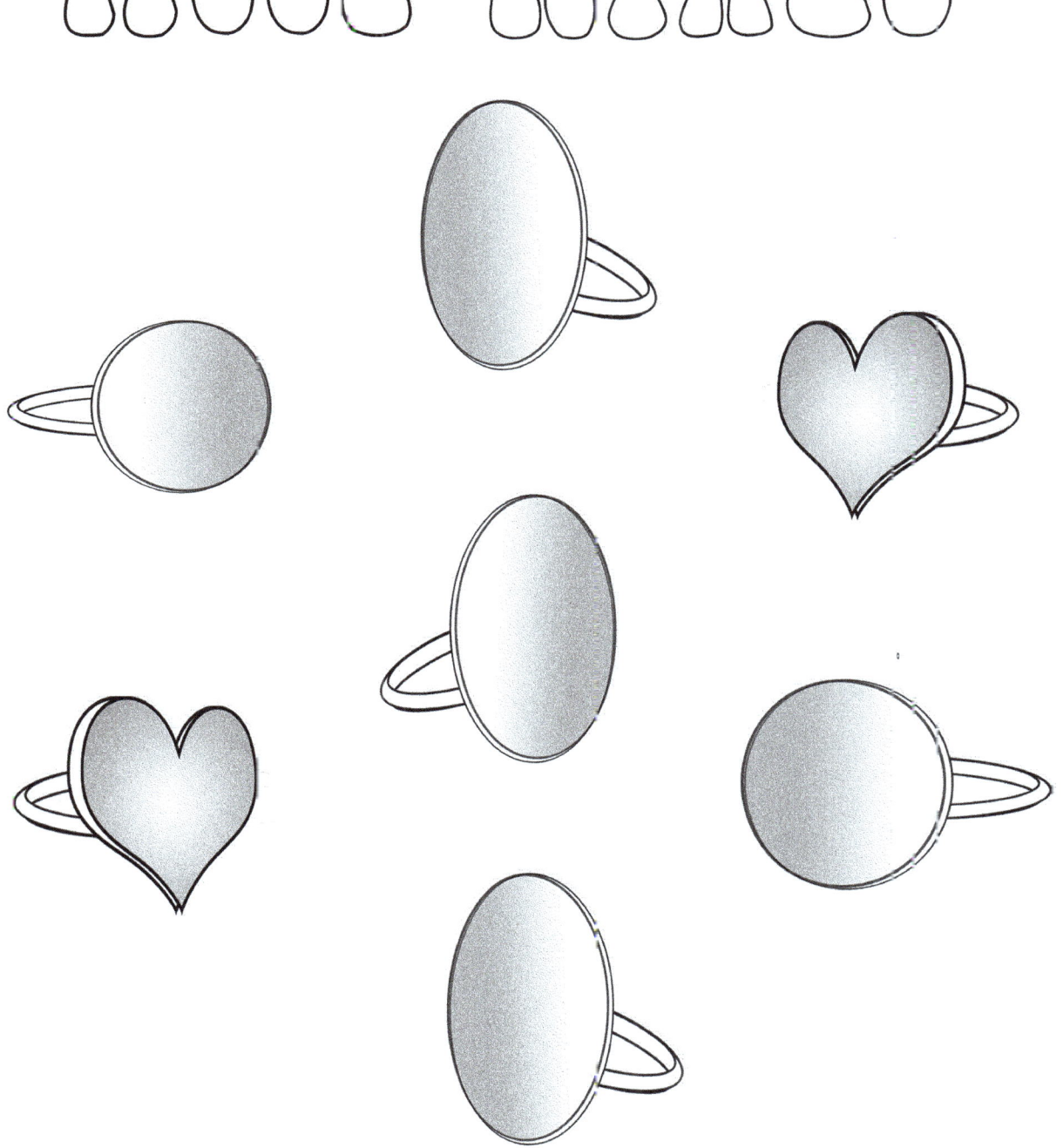

Red – lovable
Orange – worried
Yellow – imaginative
Green – calm

Blue – happy
Purple – tranquil
Black – tense

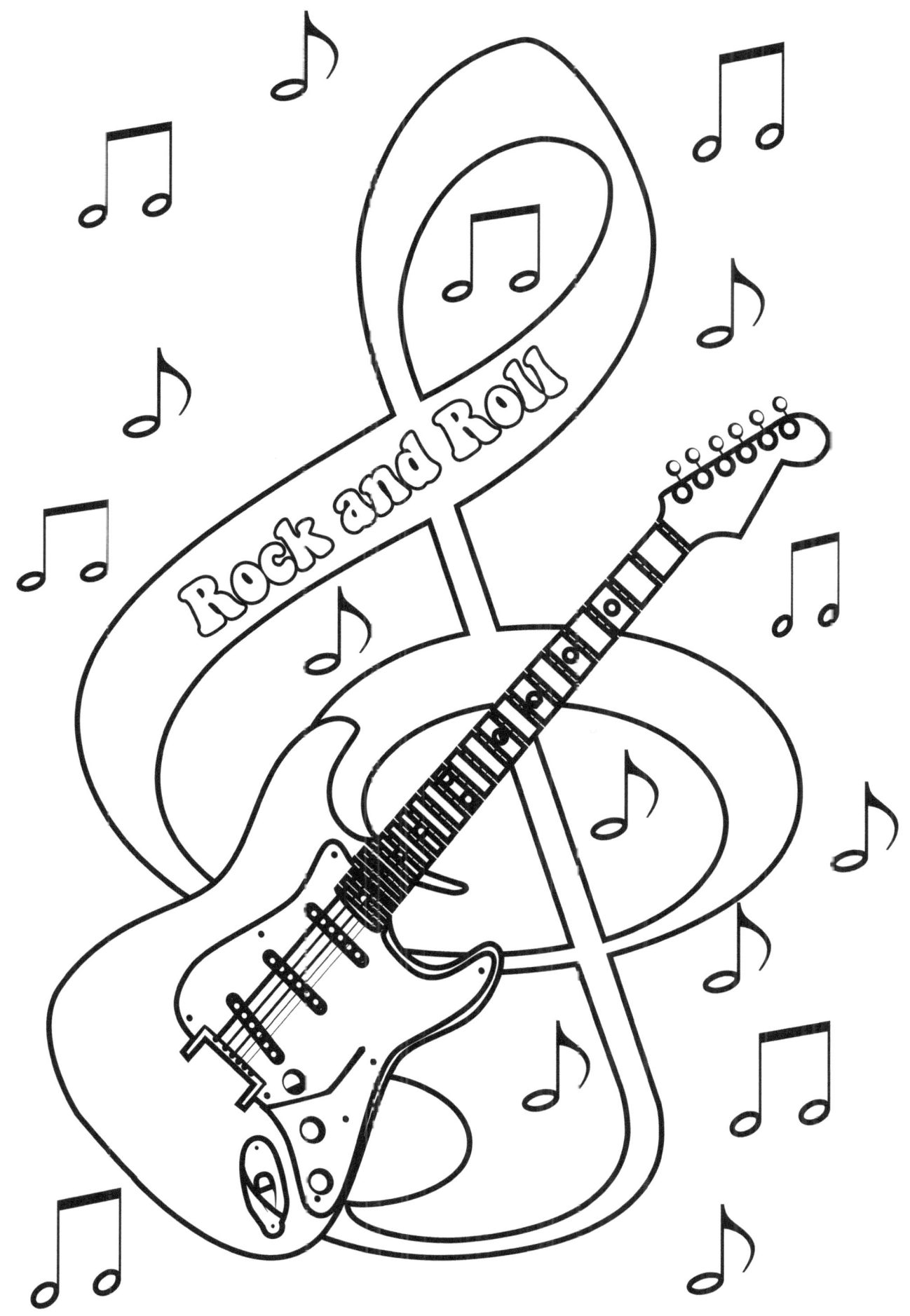

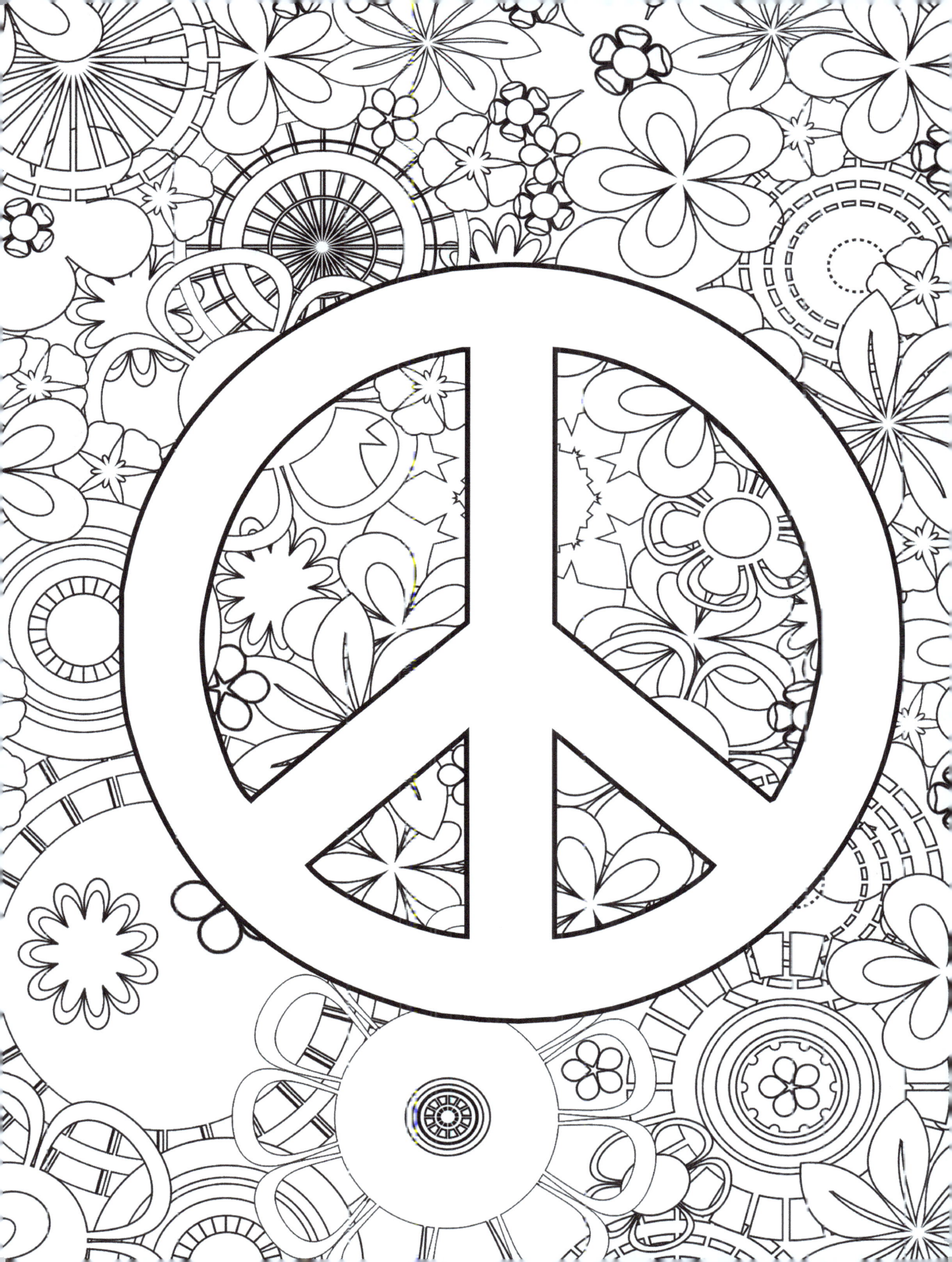

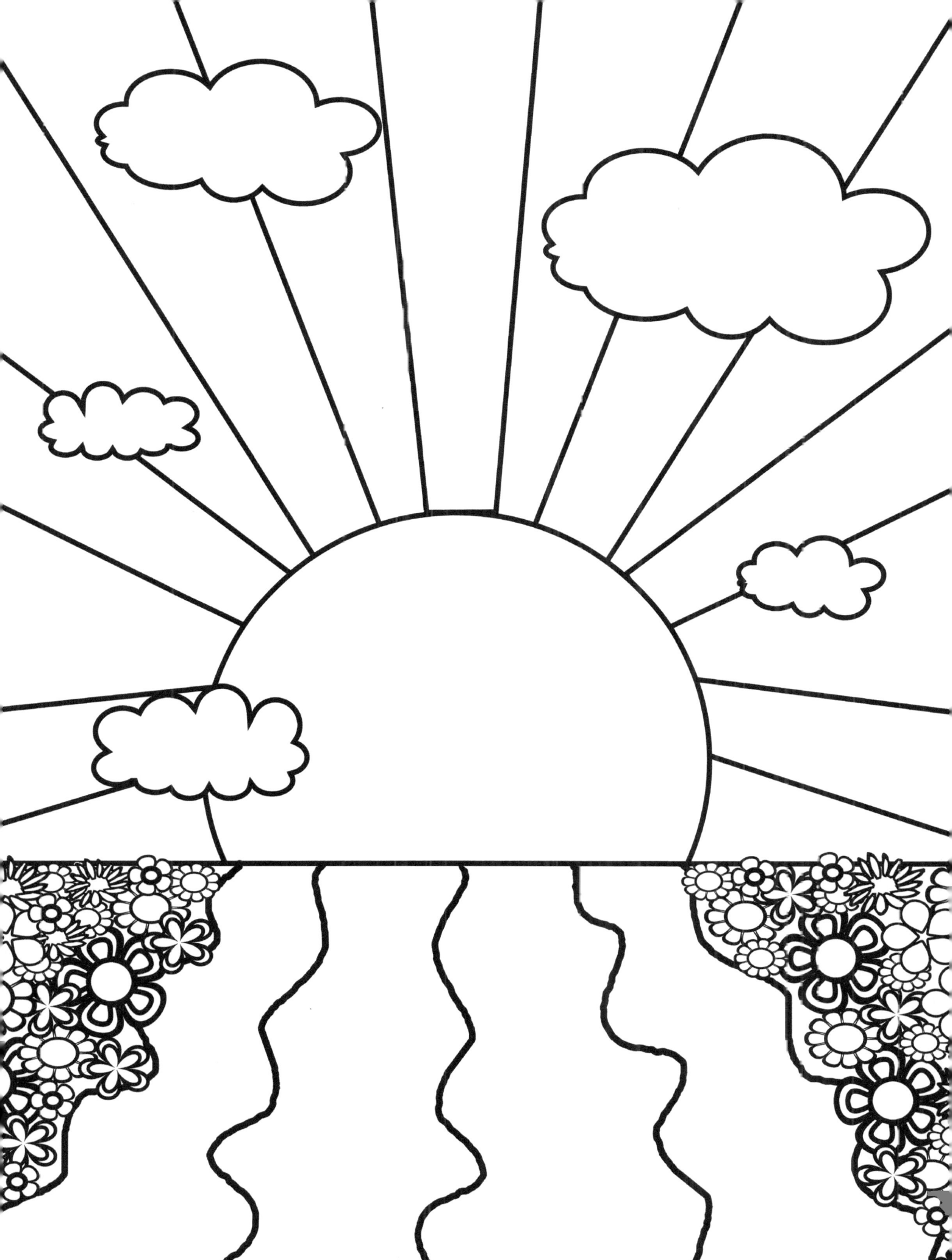

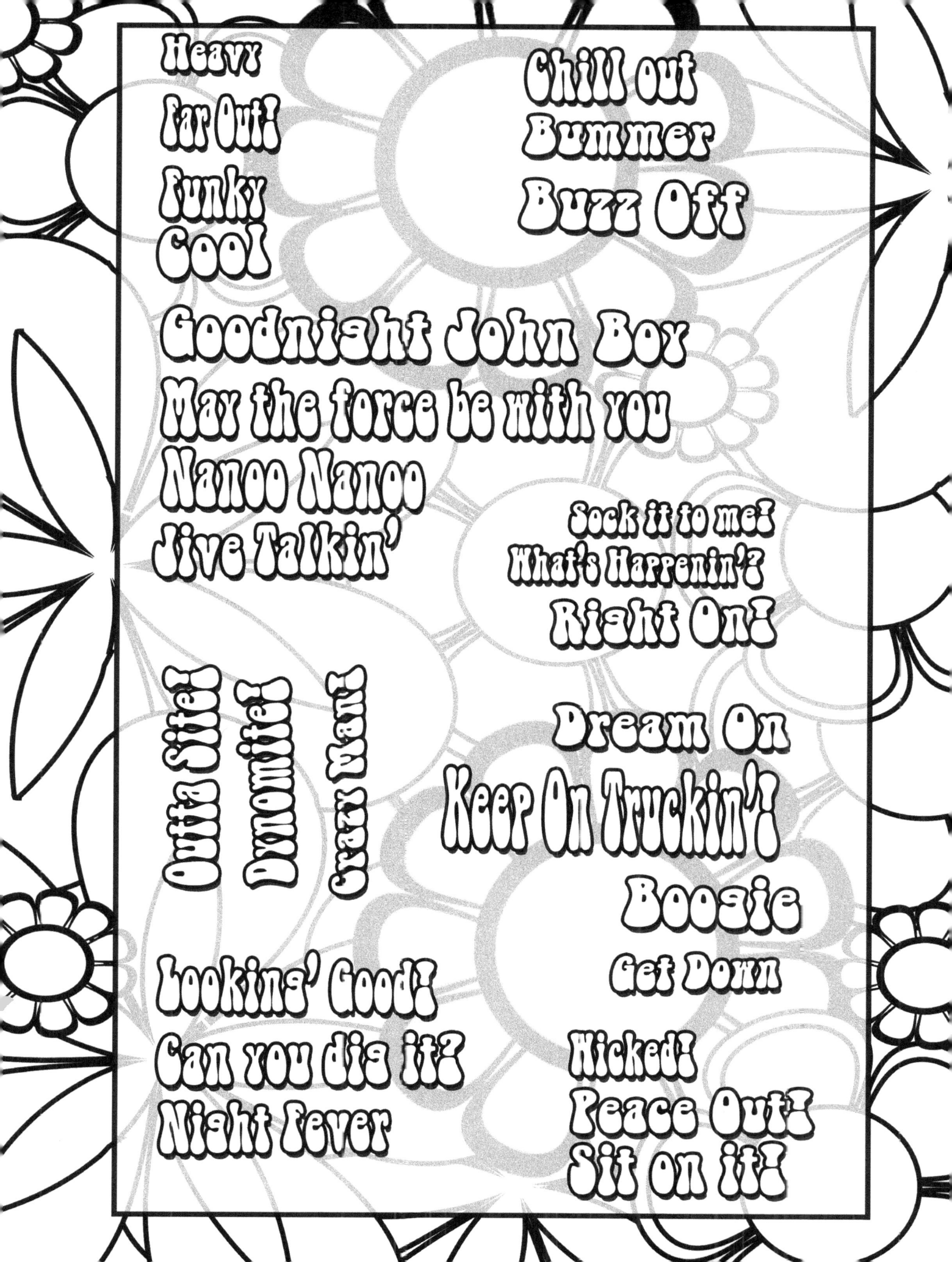

Heavy

Far Out!

Funky

Cool

Chill out

Bummer

Buzz Off

Goodnight John Boy

May the force be with you

Nanoo Nanoo

Jive Talkin'

Sock it to me!

What's Happenin'?

Right On!

Outta Site! Dynomite! Crazy Man!

Dream On

Keep On Truckin'!

Boogie

Get Down

Looking' Good!

Can you dig it?

Night Fever

Wicked!

Peace Out!

Sit on it!

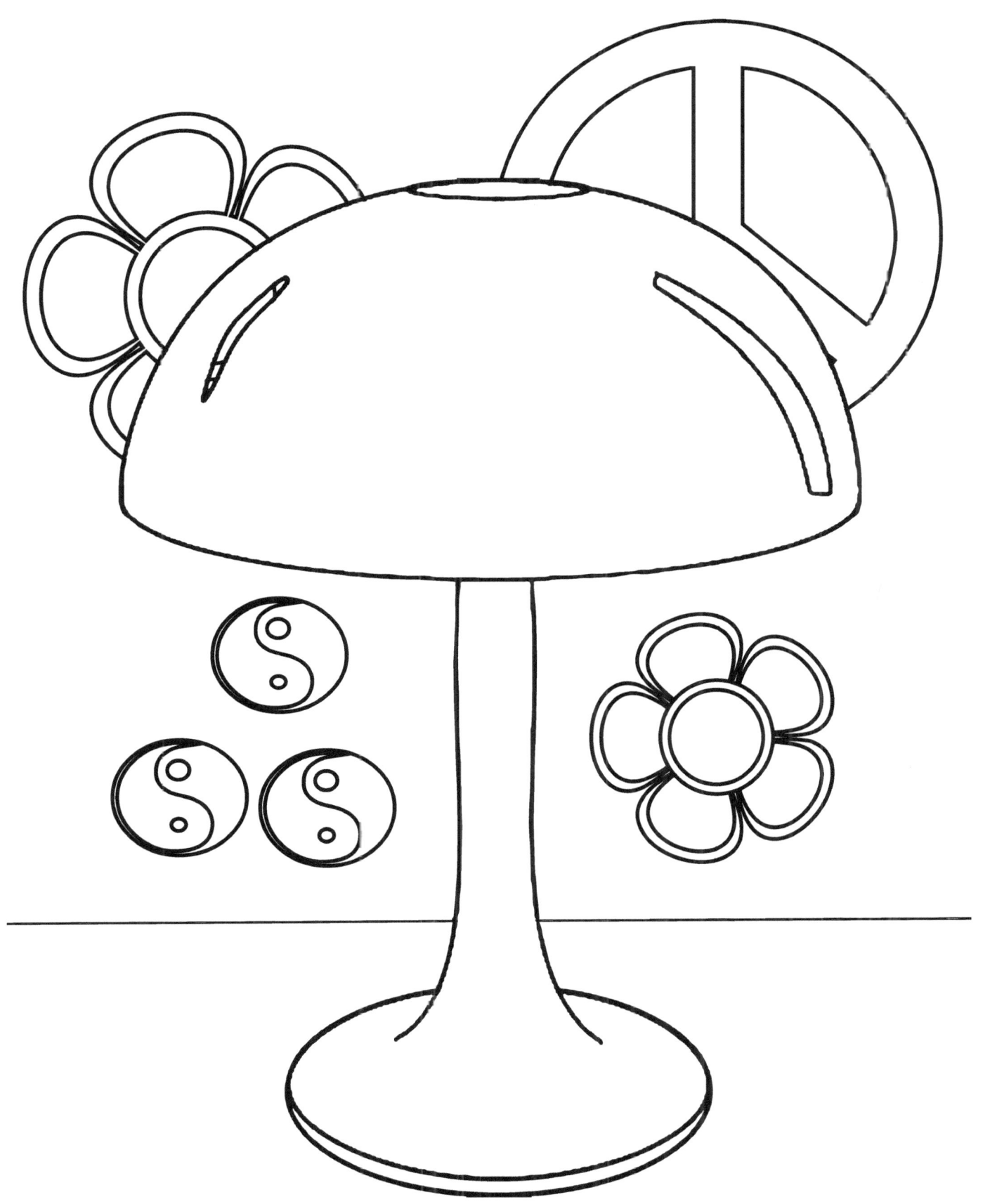

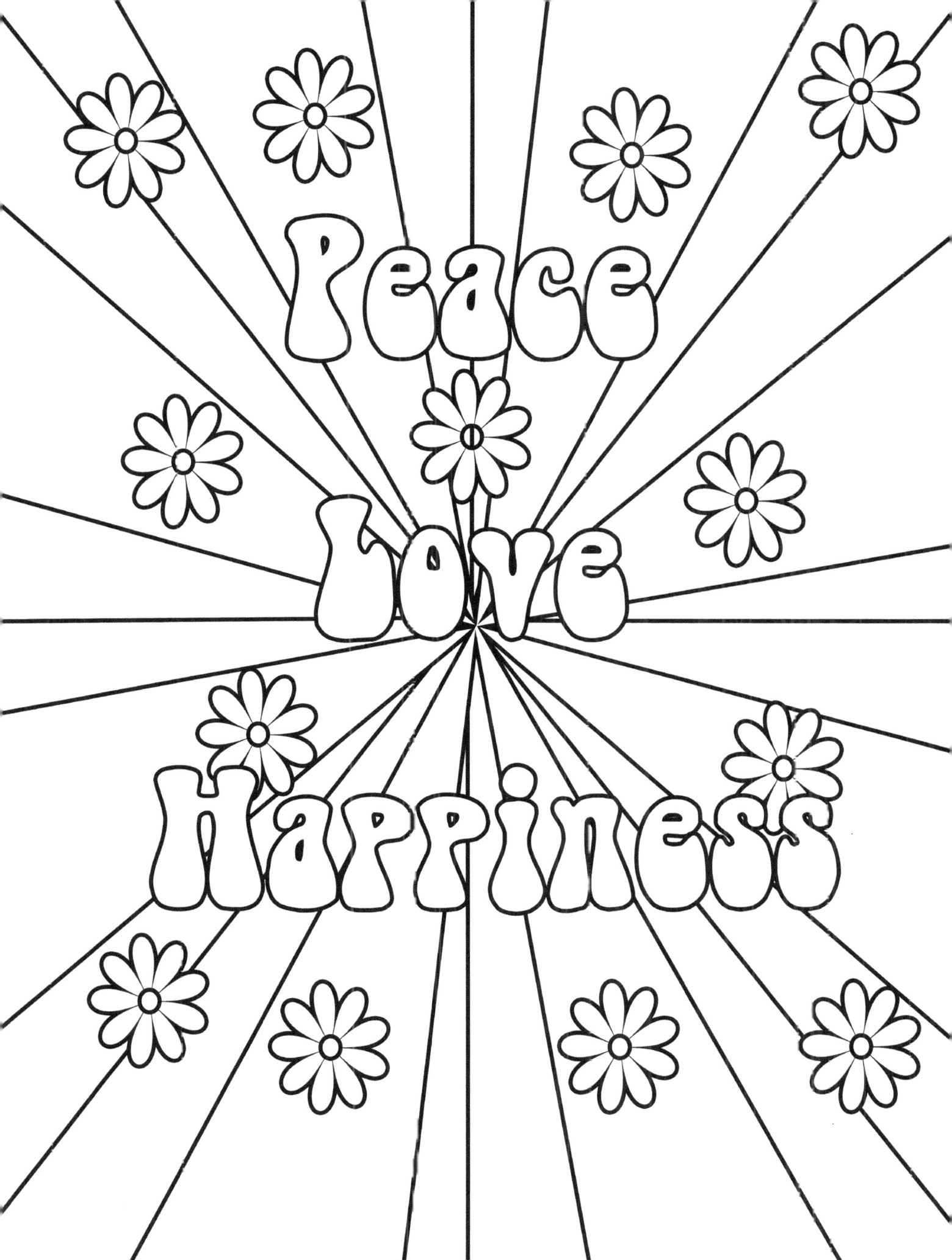

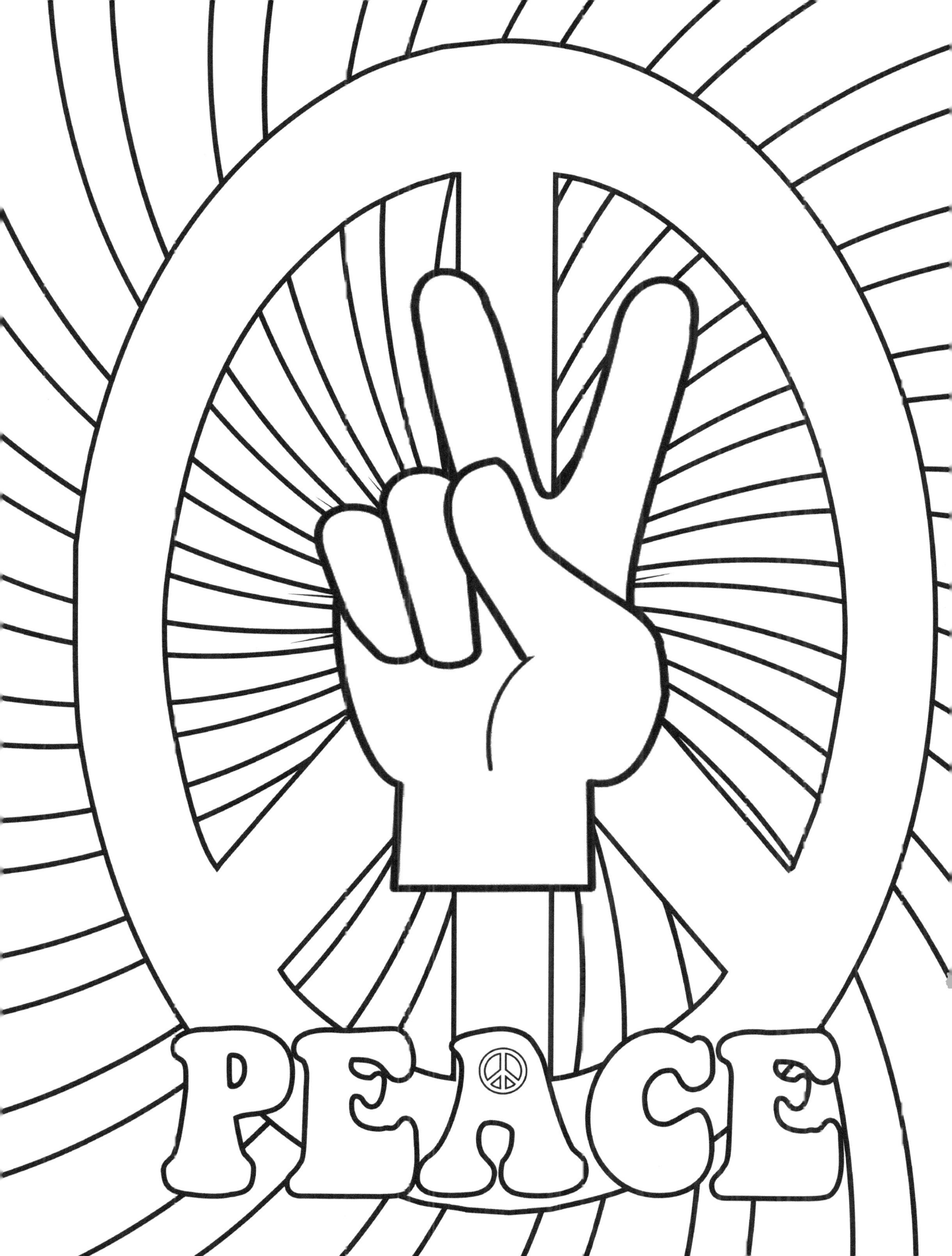

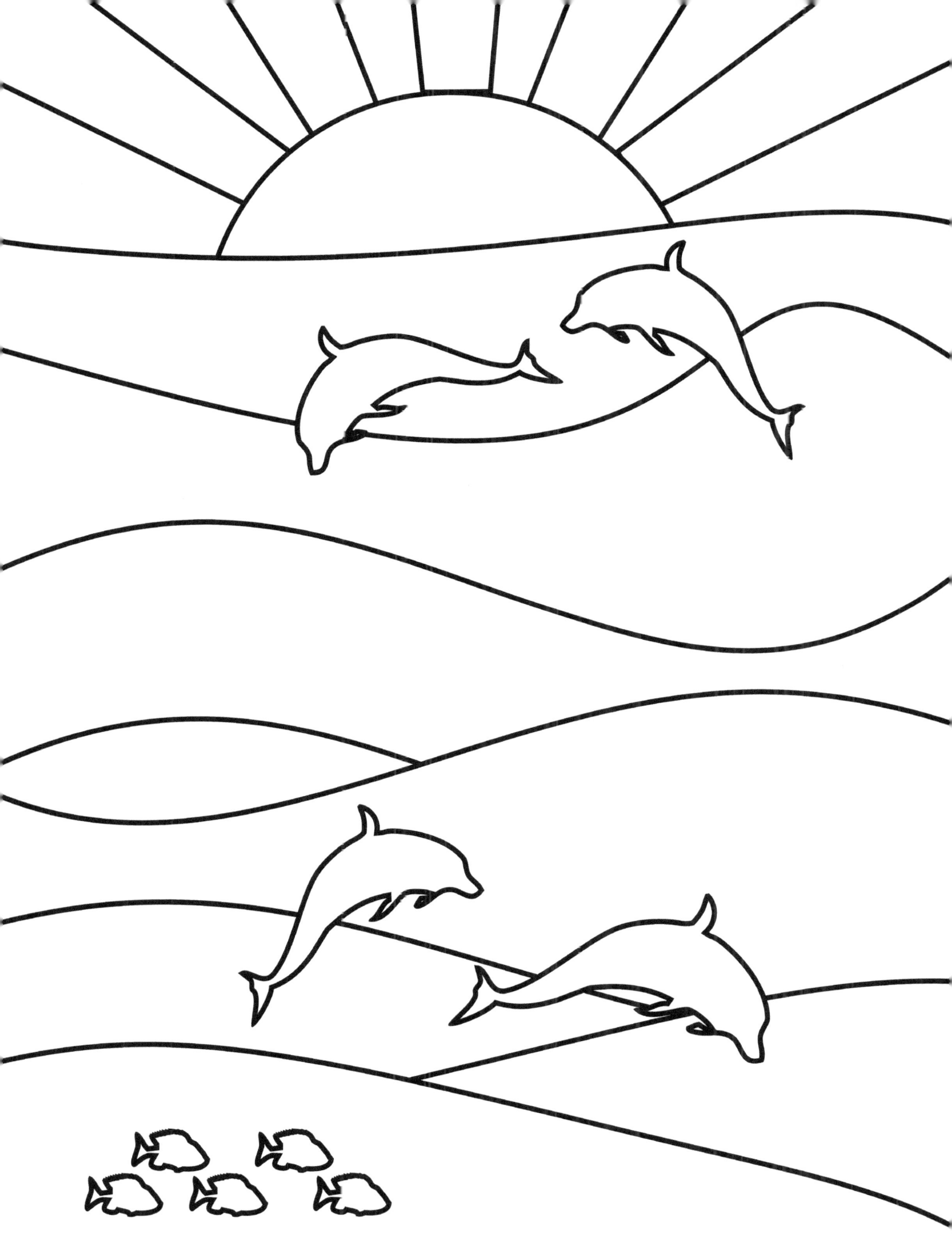

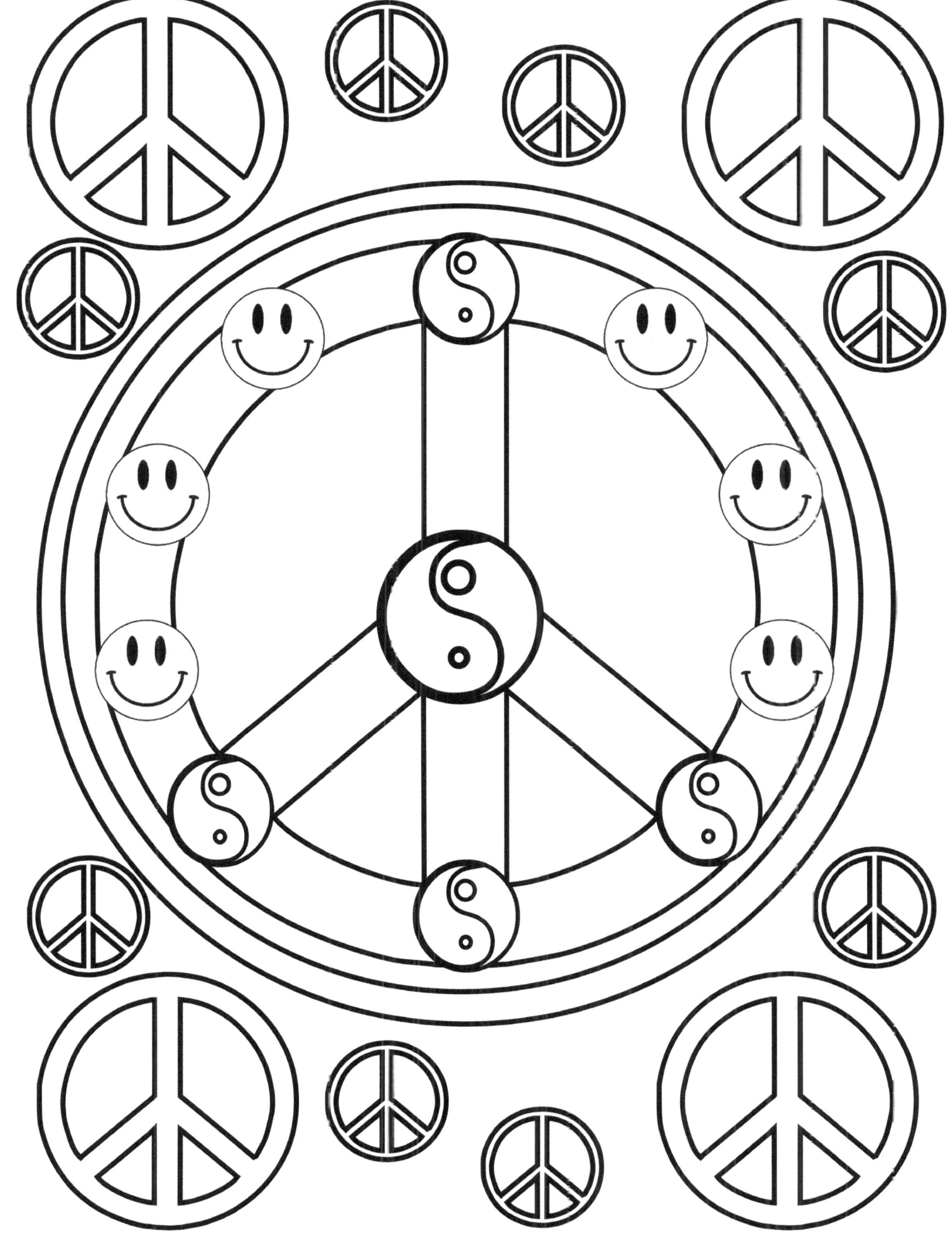

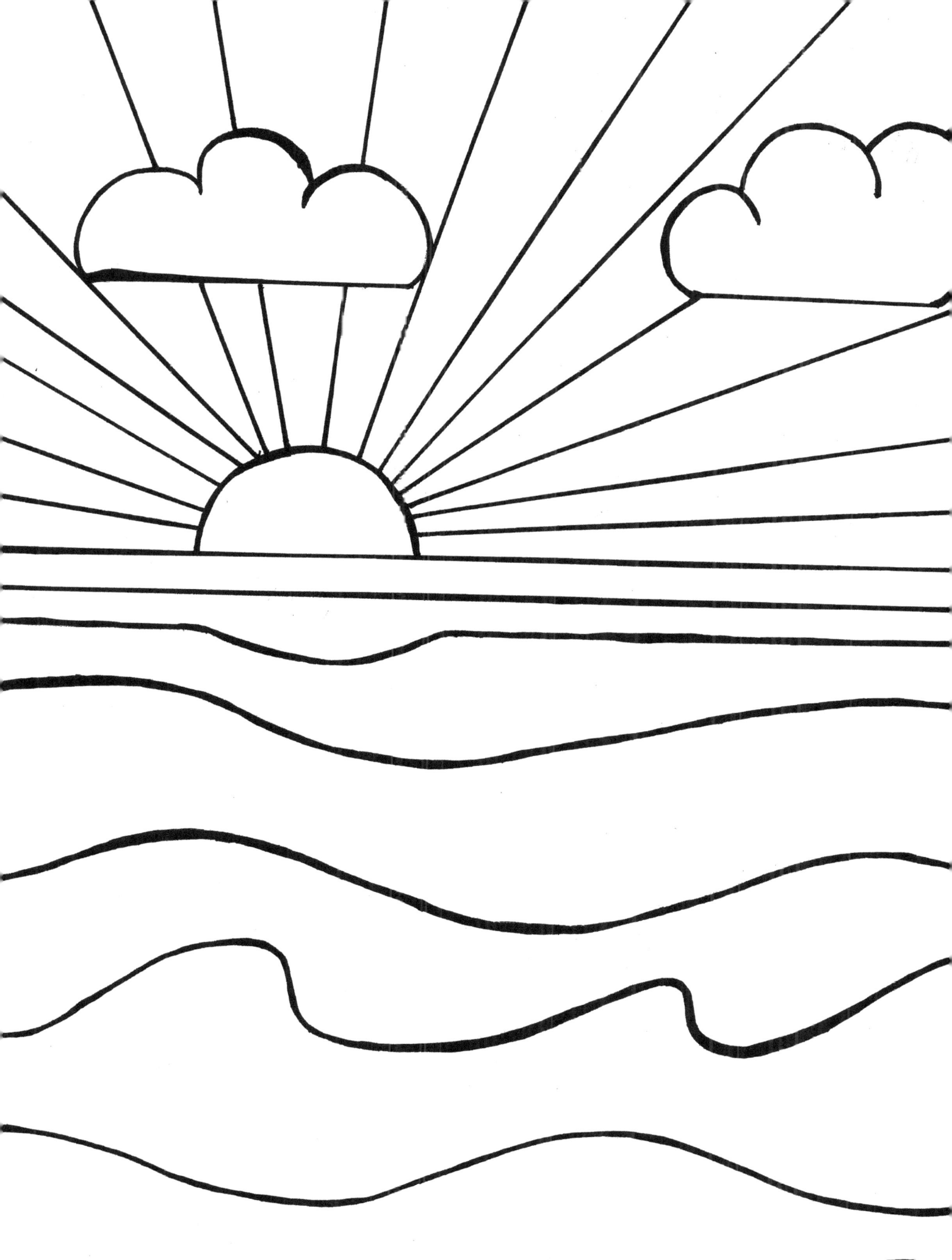

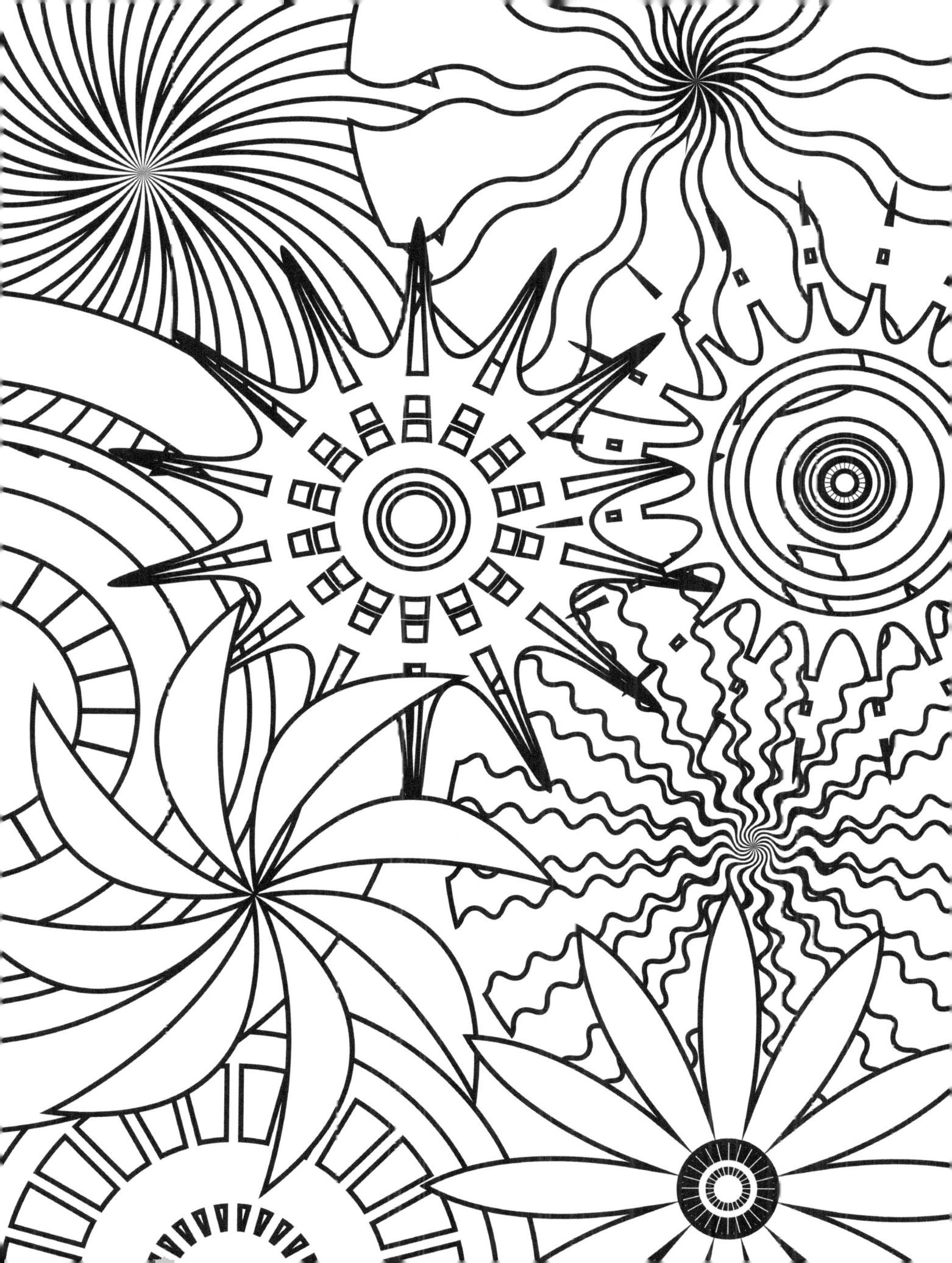

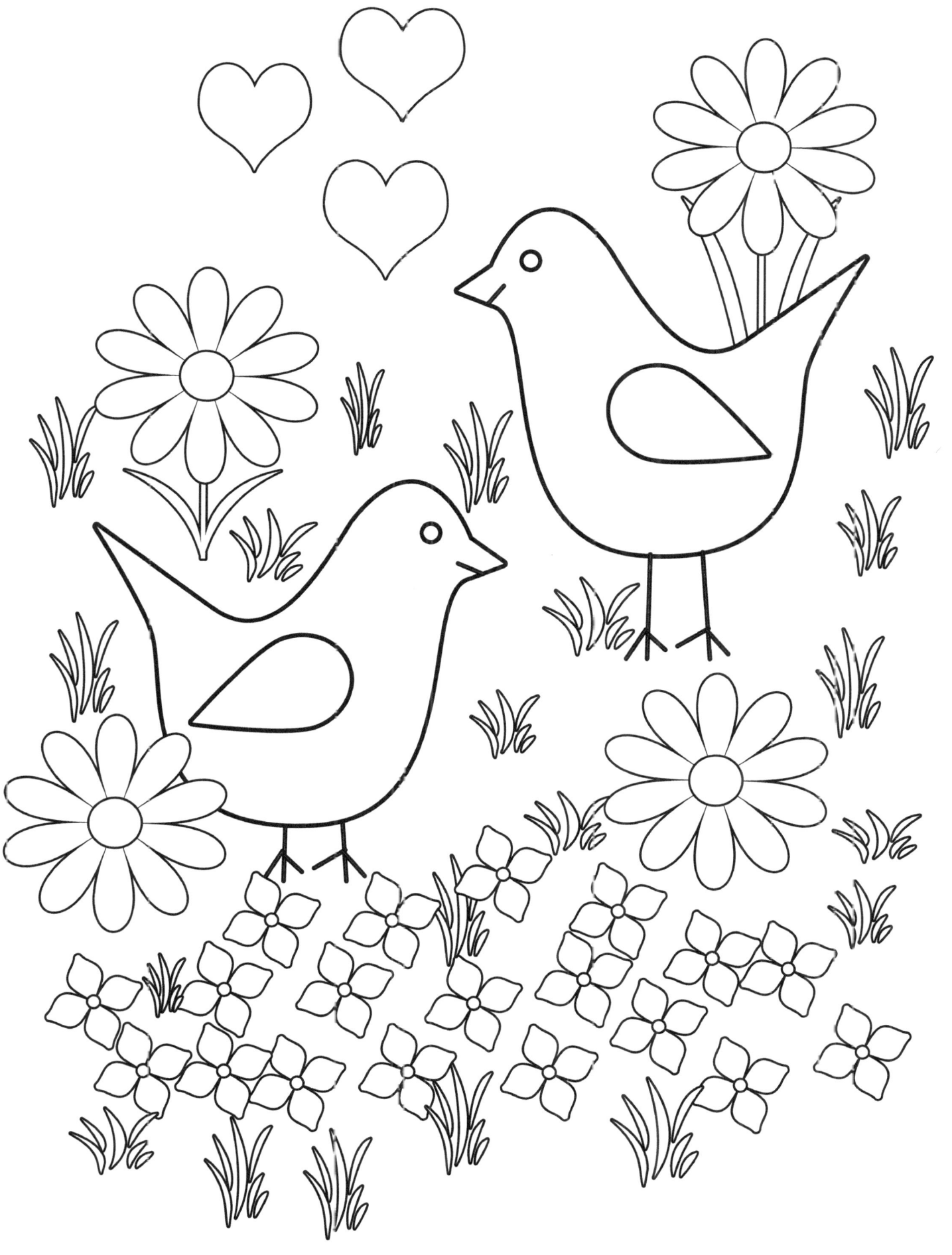

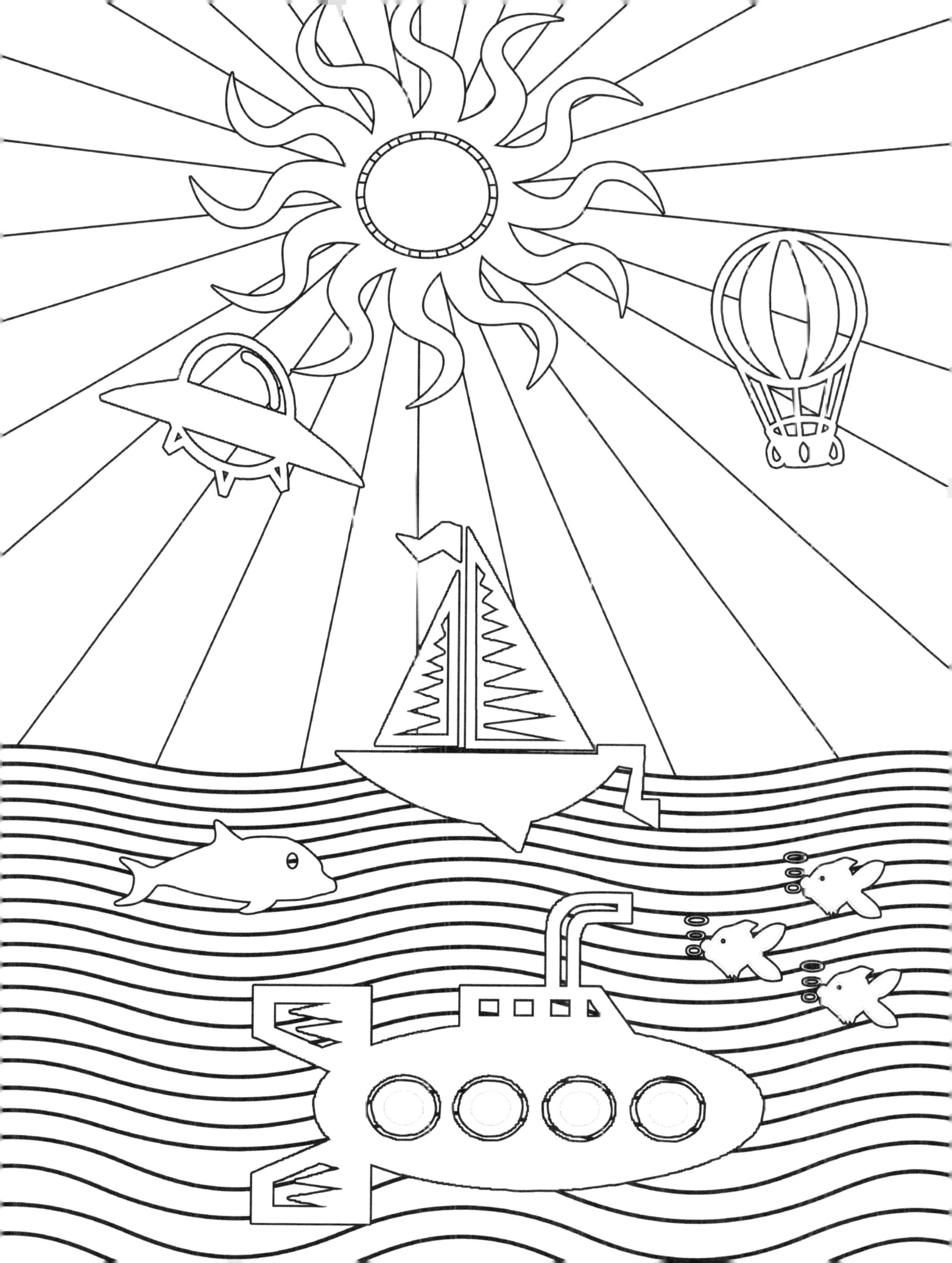

About the Author

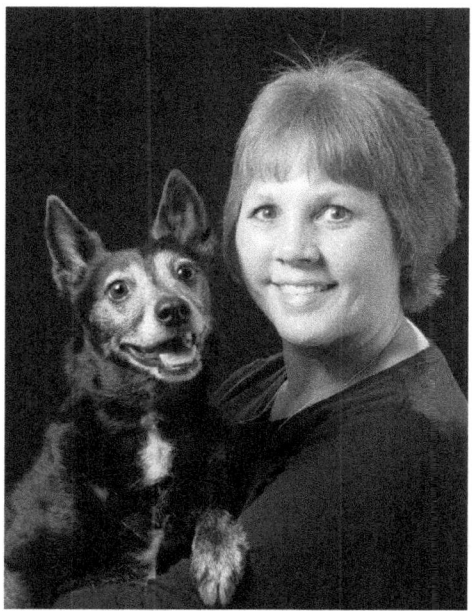

Alisa and her dog Skipper

Being a child of the 1970s herself, Alisa has always loved the bright colors and geometric designs of the late 60s and early 70s art and advertising. She fondly remembers all the cool toys that would be banned if made today, like "Clackers" and her Spirograph with straight pins to hold the paper. Many hours were spent hanging out at the skating rink in junior high, and disco dancing in high school. 1970s music is still her all-time favorite.

In junior high, Alisa discovered Flair markers. Soon after, drawings and doodles of peace signs, flowers, smiley faces, and anything bright and happy adorned her notebooks and brown paper book covers.

As the 70s progressed, Alisa became involved in other various types of art work. She sewed her own bell bottoms and made matching floppy hats to wear with them. She made macramé belts and plant hangers, dyed corn kernels to use as beads in necklaces, and tie dyed t-shirts. Her mom taught her to crochet and embroider. That led to crocheted vests and embroidered chambray shirts. She also continued to draw and paint, and discovered photography.

Alisa is now a professional photographer and digital artist. She still enjoys drawing, painting, doodling, sewing, and many types of crafts. Her goal is to bring happiness to others with her artwork and maybe take them on a little trip down memory lane to the great decade of the 70s.

www.ingramcontent.com/pod-product-compliance
Lightning Source LLC
Chambersburg PA
CBHW080542190526
45169CB00007B/2601